Successful Key Account Management In A Week

Grant Stewart

Grant Stewart has specialized in Key Accounts, Sales Management and Business Development for many companies and has run his own training and consultancy company for the last 30 years. His market-leading book on Successful Sales Management has sold over 70,000 copies.

Grant can be contacted at: grantstewart1@gmail.com

Successful Key Account Management In A Week

Grant Stewart

Teach Yourself®

First published in Great Britain in 2003 by Hodder Education.

This edition published in 2016 by John Murray Learning

First published in US in 2016 by Quercus.

Copyright © Grant Stewart 2003, 2012, 2016

The right of Grant Stewart to be identified as the Author of the Work has been asserted by him in accordance with the Copyright, Designs and Patents Act 1988.

Database right Hodder & Stoughton (makers)

The *Teach Yourself* name is a registered trademark of Hachette UK.

British Library Cataloguing in Publication Data: a catalogue record for this title is available from the British Library.

ISBN 9781473608542

eISBN 9781444159189

1

The publisher has used its best endeavours to ensure that any website addresses referred to in this book are correct and active at the time of going to press. However, the publisher and the author have no responsibility for the websites and can make no guarantee that a site will remain live or that the content will remain relevant, decent or appropriate.

The publisher has made every effort to mark as such all words which it believes to be trademarks. The publisher should also like to make it clear that the presence of a word in the book, whether marked or unmarked, in no way affects its legal status as a trademark.

Every reasonable effort has been made by the publisher to trace the copyright holders of material in this book. Any errors or omissions should be notified in writing to the publisher, who will endeavour to rectify the situation for any reprints and future editions.

Typeset by Cenveo® Publisher Services.

Printed and bound in Great Britain by CPI Group (UK) Ltd., Croydon, CR0 4YY.

John Murray Learning policy is to use papers that are natural, renewable and recyclable products and made from wood grown in sustainable forests. The logging and manufacturing processes are expected to conform to the environmental regulations of the country of origin.

Carmelite House
50 Victoria Embankment
London EC4 0DZ
www.hodder.co.uk

Contents

Foreword

Anything from Grant Stewart is bound to be of high quality, given his background, experience and wisdom. So it is of no surprise to me that this little book is a real gem, which you should read, use and keep handy for continuous reference.

The days have long gone when a traditional sales approach was sufficient for major accounts. Given the electronic availability of data, companies know instantly, for example, what products are available to them worldwide and at what price, so the most likely source of differential advantage will come from in depth supplier relationships that enable them to avoid costs, reduce costs, or add value in some way. The only way this can be done by a supplier is by knowing as much, if not more, about the customers' business than they know about their own. Only then does a supplier have a chance of developing a relationship, which will not only help the customer to avoid disadvantage (let's be clear that any supplier can do this), but to create advantage for the customer.

If you follow the straightforward guidelines in this book, your company's future is assured.

Professor Malcolm McDonald
Former Professor of Marketing and Deputy Director
Cranfield University School of Management

Introduction

Key account management is increasingly important and must keep pace with its customers as they continually develop and evolve, often resulting in increasingly sophisticated buying structures. The key account manager therefore requires a wide variety of skills in order to be successful; this is not only an important job role in its own right, it is often a stepping stone to career development, leading to more senior management jobs.

On Sunday the key account manager is encouraged to **Know your customer** as success depends on a relationship that is both rewarding and valuable. A thorough understanding of the customer is dependent on information gathered; the vital element to a strong position is the possession of knowledge.

Monday is the day to **Analyse your growth opportunities**. The competitiveness of the company must be appraised to enable the identification of sales growth opportunities and all major accounts should be compared in appeal and position to give an indication of the strategy to be adopted for customers.

Tuesday is the day to **Measure profits by account**. The key account manager is shown how to measure the profitability of major customers and to draw up league tables to enable profit improvement strategies. Less profitable customers need to be made more profitable and efforts made to grow sales with those whose profitability is higher; the customers who produce the majority of the sales are often not the same ones who produce the majority of the profit as they can make demands which reduce the supplier's margin.

On Wednesday the key account manager must **Plan for success**, building on the analysis of growth opportunities and profit measurement already considered, to result in a best judgement final plan. This plan can be used in management control, as well as to benchmark and report on performance, facilitated by a sales plan checklist.

On Thursday the key account manager is taught to **Negotiate to win-win**; success relies on understanding the difference between negotiation and selling and being able to conduct negotiations to produce a win-win situation in which the objectives of both sides are considered. The core principles of negotiation must be learned and there is great skill involved in managing the high pressure situation that is brought about by the significant costs and values to be considered.

The key account manager looks at **Control activity levels** on Friday and the monitoring of standards of performance to enable the presentation of plans and progress, allowing the measurement of success against these plans. Information management is crucial to the control cycle and the absolute success measures are the objectives covering the quantifiable goals. If standards are not being achieved, this must be diagnosed and corrected.

Finally, on Saturday the key account manager is reminded to **Manage relationships** with an introduction to the Relationship Model which describes how business with a customer changes as it moves from a transactional or short-term sales achievement, to collaboration with long-term customer value and retention.

SUNDAY

Know your customer

A successful key account manager depends on a relationship with their customer that is both rewarding and valuable. The way to achieve this relationship is explained in the following section, with emphasis placed on the importance of information gathering, to enable a thorough understanding of the customer, their business and the buying processes involved. Five categories of required information are detailed, with suggestions of pro forma given for data capture, explanations of how the information may be used, its importance and examples of practical applications. Having ascertained the facts about their customer, the key account manager is guided through learning about their policies, markets, financial performance and buying processes. The concept of a decision making unit is introduced with an explanation of the subjective and objective influences to which buying decisions made by the customer are submitted, emphasizing that the buyer does not work alone. Throughout the process, the key account manager is shown that the vital element to a strong position is the knowledge they possess. This knowledge will allow the building and maintenance of a positive relationship with the customer and the avoidance of errors which may prove costly to the business.

Information requirements

The key account manager needs to collect customer information in five categories:

Information categories

1 Customer facts
2 Customer policies
3 Customer markets and our business
4 Customer financial performance
5 Customer buying processes

Customer facts

- Locations of customer's head office, regional offices, factories, warehouses, etc.
- Names of parent company, subsidiaries and affiliates
- Number and type of outlets (if applicable)
- Planned changes to locations
- Last three years' sales turnover and profits

This information will be laid out as a pro forma with space to revise any changes of information. Accuracy of information is essential and the pro forma needs to be tailored to the specific industry in which the key account manager is operating.

For example, a key account manager selling to customers in a retail distribution business will have extra sections on areas such as:

- Square metres of space
- Average sales per square metre
- Average sales per outlet
- Break down of outlets by type and size, e.g. customer's standard outlet grading system

Alternatively, a key account manager for a computer manufacturer may collect information by end customer type, for instance, offices, retailers, manufacturers, distribution companies, service companies, etc.

Customer policies

- Customer's policy on access to customer sites and outlets
- Customer's policy on promotional and marketing support from suppliers
- Customer's policy on promotional materials allowed
- Customer's policy on entertaining and social events
- Customer's policy on pricing and discounts

The aim of collecting this type of information is to ensure that all of the key account manager's behaviours fit in with the customer's policies, thus avoiding costly mistakes.

For example, many customers are increasingly concerned about the influences on their buying departments created by suppliers' entertainment and gift policies. A key account manager who does not understand the customer's policy in this area, may ruin the relationship completely by ignoring strict guidelines laid down by the account.

Furthermore, the need to understand customer's policies is crucial in the area of contact outside head office, such as visits to customer factories, warehouses, outlets and service centres. Unauthorized visits to customer premises would harm the relationship. The key account manager needs to issue clear policy guidelines to all members of the workforce who have contact with the customer's business. This includes the sales force, delivery staff, customer administration and customer service staff.

The customer holds the key account manager responsible for the actions of all supplier staff who are in contact with the customer. An innocent mistake by a junior member of staff may impair the relationship. It is up to the key account manager to record customer policy information and to ensure that it is communicated successfully to all staff and implemented without mistakes.

Customer markets and our business

- Estimate of total purchases by customer, by market
- Sales by market, by brand or product
- Our share of customer's total business
- Customer's share of our total business

The purpose of this type of information is to answer the question 'Where are we now?' Historical sales and market information will form the springboard for analysing growth opportunities for key accounts. The information can be laid out in a pro forma:

Customer markets and our business pro forma

Year	Market category	Estimate of total purchases by customer (units and value)	Our sales to customer	% share of customer's total purchases	Customer's share % of our total sales

This pro forma can be completed for:

● Different years (trends)
● Different markets
● Different products/brands sold to each market

Customer financial performance

● Customer's return on capital employed
● Customer's return on sales
● Customer's sales in relation to capital employed
● Stock, debtor and creditor turnover
● Profit performance by product and market category

The key account manager should collect the published financial information of customers, for instance the annual report and accounts. This will give the financial summary of how the customer is performing and the key account manager can look at the trends of performance over the last two or three years to see if the customer's business is improving or deteriorating.

This knowledge will enable the key account manager to formulate profit improvement strategies for customers that empathize with the customer's profit requirements. The main areas on which such information can be collected are shown in the following table:

	Ratio	How to calculate	What it means
1	Return on capital employed	Net profit before tax/capital employed%	It measures the profits produced in relation to the total capital invested in the business. Capital employed is shareholders' funds (share capital and reserves) plus loans. Comparisons can be made with other companies in the same industry.
2	Return on sales	Net profit before tax/sales%	This measures profit after all company costs have been deducted in relation to the total sales of the company. This is effectively the customer's profit margins.
3	Capital turnover	Sales/Capital employed	This measures the speed of sales turnover in relation to the capital employed in the business. High is good.
4	Stock turnover	Stock × 365/Sales revenue	This measures how the company's inventory (stock) is turning over, expressed in number of days. The lower the number of days the better.
5	Debtor turnover	Debtors × 365/Sales revenue	This measures the customer's ability to collect payment from its customers and is expressed in number of days. Like stock turnover, debtor turnover should have a low number of days.
6	Creditor turnover	Creditors × 365/Cost of goods sold	This shows how long it takes to pay the bills of suppliers and is expressed in days. The higher the number of days, the better.

The key account manager does not need to be a financial expert – help can be sought from financial analysis books or from the internal financial department. Experience shows that understanding the customer's financial performance creates a good basis for developing strategic approaches to key customer planning and negotiation. You may wish to reduce your investment in customers whose financial performance is declining, while increasing your investment in customers whose profits are increasing.

Further information is available from a customer's stock market performance. Is its share price rising or falling? Do City financial analysts rate the customer as a buy, sell or hold, as far as the shares are concerned?

Customer buying processes

- Customer organization and buying structures
- Interests and characteristics (e.g. sports, hobbies) of customer managers
- Description of buying process
- Analysis of decision making unit (DMU)

This information section is vital because as it will guide the key account manager to develop the right quantity and quality of relationships at all relevant levels with the customer. It is well known that many key account managers fail to identify an accurate customer buying process, and fail to develop relationships with all members of the decision making unit (DMU).

A typical customer buying process would be:

- Recognition of customer needs
- Specification of products to meet needs
- Search for suppliers to meet needs
- Analysis of supplier proposals
- Evaluation of proposals and selection of suppliers
- Selection of an order routine
- Performance evaluation and feedback

These buying processes may differ according to whether the products and service needs are new, are modified from a current product or service, or are a routine repurchase.

The DMU is a core concept of key account management and can be extremely difficult to define in large accounts with many buying influences. The classic model developed by Webster and Wind (1972) identified five key groups:

1 *Users*: for example, those who influence product purchases as users.
2 *Influencers*: for instance, industrial engineers, manufacturing staff, technical personnel.
3 *Buyers*: those who place the orders may be individuals or a buying committee, and each buyer may have different characteristics affecting purchase, such as status needs, attitude to risk, willingness to negotiate.
4 *Deciders*: for example, the board of management, finance director or buying committee. A key account manager who deals only with buyers may regret a reluctance to contact deciders.
5 *Gatekeepers*: for instance, secretaries, receptionists, mail sorters, warehouse staff. Gatekeepers may be relatively junior members of staff, but key account managers may need to get them 'on side' if the other members of the DMU are to be contacted and influenced.

Each person in the DMU will have a unique profile of buying influences, which must be collected and summarized by the key account manager. These influences can be summarized under two headings:

1 *Subjective influences:* these are non-rational influences that psychologists believe have a major impact on all purchase decisions. Examples include:

- Desire for status
- Need for power
- Need for reassurance
- High or low attitude towards risk and innovation
- Need to be liked
- Need to please superiors

2 *Objective influences:* these are the rational and logical reasons for purchase and examples are:

- Price/cost
- Performance
- Reliability
- Delivery
- Service quality
- Convenience and flexibility

In practice, most buying decisions are a combination of both subjective and objective needs, and the key account manager should collect information on all possible influences of all members of the DMU. The saying 'People buy people first' is usually true. It would clearly help a supplier/customer relationship if the key account manager knew that a member of the DMU enjoyed a particular sport or hobby and this could be incorporated into the relationship process, for example, in invitations to social or sporting events.

Summary

SUNDAY

MONDAY

TUESDAY

WEDNESDAY

THURSDAY

FRIDAY

SATURDAY

The first requirement for any account manager is to know their customer. This involves spending much time and effort in data collection and assimilation to build up a full understanding of the facts, policies, markets, financial performance and buying processes relating to the customer. While the key account manager does not need to be a financial expert, the information gathered must be accurate, regularly updated and collected in an easy to access form. Customer policies must be adhered to for the avoidance of costly mistakes and it should be remembered that the customer holds the key account manager responsible for the actions of all supplier staff with whom they are in contact. Knowledge and understanding of the customer enables the formulation of profit improvement strategies for key planning and negotiation, which are facilitated by the development of the right quantity and quality of relationships at all relevant levels with the customer. Recognition of the decision making unit and its influences, whether subjective or objective, is vital; while all the information categories are important, the customer buying process is primary. If the key account manager moves on to another company, their successor should have all the core information readily to hand: knowledge is power.

Fact-check (answers at the back)

1. The key account manager needs to collect information on their customer in how many different categories?
   a) 1 ☐
   b) 5 ☐
   c) 10 ☐
   d) 20 ☐

2. It is essential that the information gathered is:
   a) accurate ☐
   b) shared with the customer ☐
   c) tailored to the specific industry ☐
   d) easy to access ☐

3. The most important of the information categories is the:
   a) customer facts ☐
   b) customer financial performance ☐
   c) customer buying processes ☐
   d) customer policies ☐

4. In examining customer policies the key account manager must include consideration of:
   a) access to customer sites and outlets ☐
   b) acceptable promotional and marketing support ☐
   c) entertaining and social events ☐
   d) whether or not they agree with the customer policies ☐

5. A key account manager's behaviour must fit in with the customer's policies:
   a) mostly ☐
   b) sometimes ☐
   c) always ☐
   d) never ☐

6. Within the key account manager's team, to whom do the customer's policy guidelines apply?
   a) it varies according to the situation ☐
   b) delivery staff ☐
   c) customer services ☐
   d) sales force ☐

7. Unauthorized visits to customer premises are likely to:
   a) make the customer feel valued ☐
   b) harm the relationship ☐
   c) be a good investment in understanding the customer ☐
   d) be beneficial to both customer and key account manager ☐

8. A key account manager will need to build a relationship with the customer's:
   a) buyer ☐
   b) secretary ☐
   c) finance department ☐
   d) none of the above ☐

9. When looking at the financial summary of the customer's performance, the key account manager needs to consider:
   a) trends over the past two or three years ☐
   b) last year's figures and projections for this year ☐
   c) estimates of sales for the next three years ☐
   d) this year's sales only ☐

10. In the formulation of profit improvement strategies the key account manager needs to consider the customer's return on capital employed. Which of the following statements are true?

a) return on capital employed measures the profits produced in relation to the total capital invested in the business ❑

b) comparisons may be made with other companies in the same industry ❑

c) return on capital employed is the only relevant consideration in determining declining or improving fortunes in a customer ❑

d) return on capital employed is one of several factors to consider in understanding the customer's financial performance ❑

SUNDAY

MONDAY

TUESDAY

WEDNESDAY

THURSDAY

FRIDAY

SATURDAY

MONDAY

Analyse your growth opportunities

To enable the identification of sales growth opportunities, the key account manager must first appraise the company's competitive situation. To assist in this process, a four-stage approach to the analysis of business growth opportunities follows, including competitive analysis, SWOT analysis, account appeal and product market matrix. A pro forma is given to illustrate the SWOT (strengths/weaknesses/opportunities/threats) analysis which may be adapted according to industry type. The use of an opportunity grid as a vital part of key account management is explained, with its purpose being to place all major accounts on a visual map to allow comparison of their appeal and position. While a standard list of these factors is not possible due to differences in industry, a comprehensive example is given. Having looked at the appeal and position, the key account manager is then shown how to score these factors, to give a weighting, or relevant importance, producing the scoring boundaries for the opportunity grid. The account grid location gives a strong indication of the strategy to be adopted for the customers. Finally, there is an explanation of the product market matrix, an effective way to position and visualize sales opportunities for major accounts and therefore to identify growth opportunities.

Analysis requirements

The key account manager needs a four-stage approach to analyse business growth opportunities:

Analysing opportunities

1 Competitive analysis

2 SWOT analysis

3 Account appeal/our position

4 Product market matrix

Competitive analysis

- Identification of competitors
- Previous actions
- Strengths/weaknesses
- Forecast plans

The first step is to identify who your competitors are for any major account's business. While this may be obvious in markets with a small number of suppliers, it becomes more complex as the number of suppliers increases. There may be competitive threats to your business with a particular customer and this may come from new sources. For example, an overseas competitor attacking your core market or attacks from new entrants into an existing market.

One example is the food distribution business in any country, which could be changed overnight by the entry of one of the USA giants with an aggressive buying and pricing policy.

A second example is the financial services market, where traditional bank and insurance company suppliers could face new competitors from other retail fields, such as non-food and food retailers.

These competitors need to be analysed in terms of strengths and weaknesses. Some may have financial strengths, but little understanding of your market, whereas others may be relatively small companies, but with strongly focused expertise in your core markets. Their plans are never published in advance and you will need to look at their previous actions and behaviour to forecast their likely strategy and action plans.

Failure to anticipate a competitive attack on one of your major customers could lead to a disastrous loss of business in a very short period of time.

Strengths/weaknesses/ opportunities/threats (SWOT)

- Identify key areas for SWOT Analysis
- Identify your strengths
- Recognize weaknesses
- Highlight likely opportunities
- Recognize real threats

The SWOT analysis has been an important corporate analysis tool for many years and its application is appropriate for key account management.

The topic areas of the analysis should reflect their importance in the eyes of major customers. The following example of a SWOT pro forma is taken from a retail food distribution supplier. Topic headings will vary according to industry and while this example covers eight topics, there is no limit to the number of topics that can be analysed.

Strengths/weaknesses/opportunities/threats

	Strengths	Weaknesses	Opportunities	Threats
Product range				
Product quality				
Branding				
Pricing/Terms				
Distribution/ Listings (% outlets stocked)				
Service (delivery, sales)				
Promotions				
Merchandising				

The important point about a SWOT analysis is to express strengths and weaknesses against competition. It is not a strength if the competition is also strong in that area. For example, your company's product quality may be excellent, but if major competitors provide a similar product quality, then this is not a competitive strength.

Account appeal/our position

● Create an opportunity grid
● Analyse customer appeal factors
● Analyse the strengths of your position
● Position accounts on opportunity grid

The creation of an opportunity grid is a vital part of key account management – it forms the basis of the account strategy and plan.

The purpose of the opportunity grid is to place all of your company's major accounts on to a visual map. This works as follows:

Opportunity Grid

	100	200	300	400	
	3	2	1	High	
				300	
	6	5	4	Medium	Appeal
				200	
	9	8	7	Low	
				100	
	Weak	Medium	Strong		

Position

The key account manager needs to analyse the appeal and position factors, in order to score each account and place them on the grid. Every industry is different, so there can be no standard list of appeal and position factors.

However, the following is a comprehensive example drawn from a supplier in the retail food distribution business.

The scoring boundaries used above (100–400) are taken from the example company used. The grid numbers (1–9) are explained at the end of this section.

Account appeal factors

1 *Market factors*	
Volume turnover	
Rate of growth	
Range stocked	
Access	Access to those parts of the key account needed to achieve your objectives. There will be two main areas: 1 Middle management 2 Branches
Support	Of our brands by account.
2 *Financial factors*	
Demand for discount	
Distribution policy	This could be in the form of warehouse delivery to branches, direct distribution or third-party supply. The important thing is how effective the operation is, not which of these three is in operation.
Prompt payment	
Instant volume ability	Is the account able to take deliveries of large volumes at short notice and pay for them?
3 *Environmental factors*	
Provision of information	How willing or able is the account to supply the kind of information you need for effective business planning?
Buyer relationship	Quality of interpersonal relationship with key account manager and those able to take decisions and implement policy on the key account side.

Your position factors

Brand strength in account	
Product range stocked	
Merchandising support	In the sphere of pack facings and point-of-sale material.
Market share	Your share of that particular key account business.

Competitor activity	In the sphere of promotional activity.
In-store furniture	The proportion supplied by you as opposed to other manufacturers.
Pull through ability	This factor refers to the ability of the account to implement and pull through promotional business development plans. In all probability, two main areas will need investigation: 1 Middle management 2 The point of sale
Distribution/Delivery effectiveness	This is the measure of efficiency of the key account to have the correct brands in appropriate volumes always available at the point of sale.
Promotional/Pricing flexibility	Is the key account able to meet our needs in these respects?
Company awareness	The key account manager's awareness and understanding of the complete key account operation, its aspirations, successes, failures, strengths and weaknesses.
Complication factors	Disruption of business plans for whatever reason – management, inflexibility of varying systems etc.
Service relationship	Strength of your position with account.

Each of these factors should be scored. It is best to weight each factor in importance by allocating 100 points to each category of appeal and position. Score each factor by using a system of, for example, marks from one to four. The weighted average score is achieved by multiplying the weighting (relative importance) by the score. If we use a four-point scoring system as an example, the maximum in each of the two categories will be 4 × 100 = 400. This will make it easy to produce the scoring boundaries for the nine boxes in the opportunity grid, thus reducing the subjectivity involved in the scoring. If we take the appeal/position factors as above, the weighted average score for one account might be as follows:

Account appeal				Our position/Strength			
1 *Market factors*	Weight	Score	Total		Weight	Score	Total
Volume turnover	20	3	60	Brand strength in account	18	3	54
Rate of growth	12	2	24	Product range stocked	10	3	30
Range stocked	10	3	30	Merchandising support	6	2	12
Access	6	4	24	Market share	12	3	36
Support	6	2	12	Competitor activity	7	2	14
2 *Financial factors*				In-store furniture	4	2	8
Demand for discount	10	1	10	Pull through ability	4	3	12
Distribution policy	10	2	20	Distribution/Delivery effectiveness	15	3	45
Prompt payment	4	4	16	Promotional/ Pricing flexibility	10	2	20
Instant volume ability	10	3	30	Company awareness	4	4	16
3 *Environmental factors*				Complication factors	4	4	16
Provision of information	4	3	12	Service relationship	6	2	12
Buyer relationship	8	2	16				
TOTAL	**100**		**254**		**100**		**275**

In the example used here, this account scores 254 for appeal, and 275 for position. This would place the account in the middle/right portion of box 5 on the grid.

At the end of this important analytical process the key account manager can see all of the accounts placed in the nine grid boxes. Although there can be some exceptions, the usual way to use the opportunity grid is as follows:

Account grid Location	Opportunities	Strategy
Boxes 1, 2 and 4	Strong position/appeal	Defend/improve
Boxes 3, 5 and 7	Selective opportunities	Build and develop
Boxes 6, 8 and 9	Weak position/appeal	Milk/withdraw

Product market matrix

- Market size estimates
- Product sales by market
- Product/market trends
- Opportunity areas

The product market matrix is an effective way to position and visualize the sales opportunities for major accounts.

The matrix can be used in a variety of ways and the following example shows how it works.

The product market matrix

£000	Market 1	Market 2	Market 3	Product trend	TOTAL
Product 1	100 / 60	2000 / 80	400 / 150	Increasing 33% p.a.	2500 / 290
Product 2	500 / 30	1000 / 100	2000 / 100	Decreasing 7% p.a.	3500 / 230
Product 3	1200 / 100	2400 / 200	1600 / 40	Increasing 2% p.a.	5200 / 340
Market trend	Static	Growing 14% p.a.	Increasing 3% p.a.		
TOTAL	1800 / 190	5400 / 380	4000 / 290		11200 / 860

P / A	P = Potential purchases, i.e. market size. A = Actual purchases from us. p.a. = Per annum.

The word 'market' can have various meanings, including different countries, sales regions, end user types or industries.

The product categories can be individual items, product groups or broad generic categories. The market/product boxes can be further subdivided to show the last two years' performance.

Independent market research may help to identify market sizes for particular accounts, but this can be extrapolated from market share estimates. Moreover, many customers are happy to give market size estimates for their category business.

The product market matrix can be used by the key account manager to identify growth opportunities, or at very least to provide a basis for further investigation. In the above example, Product 1 in Market 2 would be a good potential opportunity area – the product is increasing at 33% per annum, the market is growing 14% per annum and the share of total business in that market is well below the average level. There may, of course, be good reason for this under-performance, but this simple analysis method can produce very good growth opportunities.

Summary

The sales opportunities for each account must be considered carefully by the key account manager. The four analysis requirements to understand business growth opportunities are: competitive and SWOT analyses, account appeal and product market matrix. The competitive analysis allows for the identification of competitors, examination of previous actions, consideration of strengths and weaknesses and forecast planning. In choosing the topic areas of analysis for SWOT, the key account manager must examine their own company to identify strengths, recognize weaknesses, highlight likely opportunities and understand real threats. In consideration of account appeal and the key account manager's own position in relation to the customer's business, an opportunity grid is a useful tool. With this grid it is possible to reduce subjectivity in analysing customer appeal factors relative to the strength of the manager's own position. This visual map gives a strong indication of the opportunities available and therefore of the strategy to adopt for each account. Finally, the product market matrix effectively positions the sales opportunities for major accounts, given consideration of market size estimates, product sales by market, product/market trends and areas of opportunity. At the very least, this will provide a basis for further investigation by the key account manager.

SUNDAY

MONDAY

TUESDAY

WEDNESDAY

THURSDAY

FRIDAY

SATURDAY

Fact-check (answers at the back)

1. How many stages are involved in analysing business growth opportunities?
   a) one ❏
   b) two ❏
   c) three ❏
   d) four ❏

2. Complete the phrase. Product market...
   a) format ❏
   b) template ❏
   c) matrix ❏
   d) pattern ❏

3. Competitors need to be analysed in terms of:
   a) strengths and weaknesses ❏
   b) the size of their company ❏
   c) financial position only ❏
   d) the plans they publish ❏

4. SWOT is an acronym for strengths, weaknesses, opportunities and...
   a) timescales ❏
   b) threats ❏
   c) teamwork ❏
   d) trials ❏

5. How many topics should be considered in a SWOT analysis?
   a) as few as possible ❏
   b) five ❏
   c) eight ❏
   d) there is no limit ❏

6. With reference to an opportunity grid, which of the following statements apply?
   a) the list of appeal and position factors is the same in every industry ❏
   b) it places the company's major accounts on a visual map ❏

   c) there is no standard list of appeal and position factors ❏
   d) there is no potential for comparison between accounts ❏

7. In considering account appeal factors which of the following are applicable?
   a) market factors ❏
   b) financial factors ❏
   c) environmental factors ❏
   d) it varies from time to time ❏

8. The word 'market' can have various meanings, including:
   a) different countries ❏
   b) sales regions ❏
   c) industries ❏
   d) none of the above ❏

9. Product categories in the product market matrix can be
   a) of little relevance to the scoring ❏
   b) individual items ❏
   c) product groups ❏
   d) broad generic categories ❏

10. The product market matrix can be used by the key account manager
    a) to identify growth opportunities ❏
    b) as a stand alone tool to look at sales opportunities ❏
    c) to provide a basis for further investigation ❏
    d) to show under performance ❏

TUESDAY

Measure profits by account

The most important customers for a company in terms of sales may not be the most important in terms of profit. In this section, the key account manager is shown how to measure the profitability of major customers; the relationship between sales and profits is the impetus for developing key account management as a separate part of the sales force. There are many benefits of profit analysis and a full explanation of how to achieve such an analysis, involving the drawing up of a full profit and loss account, follows. Costs attributable to customers must be considered, although some of these can only be attributed by estimation and sampling methods. It is shown that profitability league tables may then be drawn up between customers, to compare those in the same market segments as well as to make comparisons between different market segments. The significance of this information is that it enables profit improvement strategies which must be used to inform the key account manager's ongoing negotiation process with each major customer. Finally there are three exercises to check understanding of financial fluency and awareness, with answers and explanations given.

Comparing sales and profits

The impetus for developing key account management as a separate part of sales force management was the 80:20 rule. This means that, in general, 80 per cent of a company's sales turnover will come from 20 per cent of customers (known as the Pareto statistical distribution).

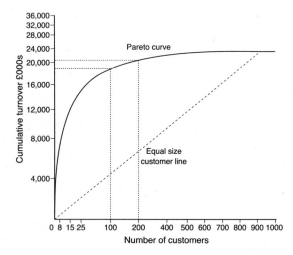

Eighty per cent of a company's profits will also come from around 20 per cent of its customers, but these are generally not the same 20 per cent who produce most of the sales. This is because major customers can demand and obtain better levels of price, promotional discounts and service levels, thus reducing the supplier's profits considerably.

In a recent analysis carried out for a client, not one of their top 25 customers in terms of sales turnover featured in their top 25 league table of customers in terms of per cent profit. A comparison can be made as follows:

Customer	% of your sales turnover	% of your profits
1	22	16
2	16	14
3	11	5
4	8	10

This type of analysis indicates that the key account manager should try to make less profitable customers more profitable and try to grow sales turnover with customers whose profitability is higher.

The following real example shows two customers in the same market category who produce very different levels of profitability to the supplier.

	% of combined sales turnover	% of combined gross margin	% of combined net profit
Customer 1	45.6%	40.1%	6.3%
Customer 2	54.4%	59.9%	93.7%
	100.0%	100.0%	100.0%

This example shows that two customers with similar sales volume start to move apart at the gross margin level and are distinctly different at the net profit level. Customer 2 is much more profitable to this supplier because it buys more profitable products, at higher price levels and at lower servicing costs than Customer 1.

Analysing major customer profitability

Analysing the profitability of major customers is usually carried out by the financial department. The process involves attributing costs at a number of different levels to each major customer, so that a full profit and loss account can be drawn up. Typical costs attributable to customers would be as follows:

Costs attributable to customers

● Cost of sales
● Commissions
● Sales calls
● Key account management time
● Order processing costs

- Promotional costs
- Non-standard packaging and unitization
- Dedicated inventory holding costs
- Dedicated warehousing costs
- Material handling costs
- Transport costs
- Documentation/communication
- Returns/refusals
- Credit taken

Some of these costs can only be attributed by estimation and sampling methods. For example, time spent by the sales force servicing each major customer can be calculated by completion of sample time sheets, which are then applied to the hourly cost of each salesperson. Provided that the calculations are applied consistently between each major customer, comparisons can be made. A typical profit and loss account by a customer would look like the table below:

	Customer A	
	£000	%
Standard price (excluding tax)	70,000	100
Manufacturing costs	40,600	58
Maximum gross contribution	**29,400**	**42**
Total discounts	16,100	23
Actual gross contribution	**13,300**	**19**

SUNDAY
MONDAY
TUESDAY
WEDNESDAY
THURSDAY
FRIDAY
SATURDAY

	Customer A	
Delivery costs:		
200–999.9 drop size	1,050	1.5
1,000+ drop size	1,050	1.5
Total Distribution Costs	2,100	3
Distributed Contribution Selling costs:	11,200	16
Key account	35	0.05
Regional	700	1
Merchandising	315	0.45
Total selling costs	1,050	1.5
Selling contribution	10,150	14.5
Extended credit cost	1,960	2.8
Office administration	210	0.3
Net contribution	7,980	11.4
Allocated overheads	4,270	6.1
Net profit	3,710	5.3

In this example, the definitions are as follows:

Standard price	List price of products bought by that customer multiplied by sales volume.
Manufacturing costs	Direct product costs (materials, labour, packaging) of product mix bought by that customer.
Discounts	Total discounts given to that customer, which can be broken down by different types if required.
Delivery costs	Costs analysed by delivery size.
Selling costs	Time costs, estimated for all sales personnel servicing this account.
Extended credit cost	Cost of special payment terms give in to this account.
Office administration	Estimate of administrative time costs involved in servicing this account.
Allocated overheads	This is all the head office and central overheads, which are usually allocated in relation to sales turnover.

Application of customer profitability information

It is now possible to produce profitability league tables to compare major customers in the same market segments. Comparisons can also be made between different market segments, for example, comparing wholesale major customers with direct customers and sales agents.

League tables can be presented in striking visual format with the help of software packages. Armed with this vital information, the key account manager can analyse each major account for profit improvement opportunities. Alternatives can be brainstormed and their financial impact measured.

The alternatives listed below can all have a significant impact on profit improvement:

Profit improvement strategies

- Increase sales of more profitable products
- Achieve sales in new outlets
- Improve merchandising impact
- Increase sales in more profitable geographical regions
- Introduce new products

- Promote sales more effectively
- Produce customer's own brand products
- Increase or reduce selling prices
- Increase sales volume
- Reduce customer discounts and promotional allowances
- Reduce sales force servicing costs
- Reduce customer credit period
- Negotiate improved contractual terms

In some cases, the key account manager can afford to invest more in profitable accounts or reduce attention given to less profitable accounts. This profitability information is of great importance during the ongoing negotiation process with each major customer.

Experience of working on consultancy and training projects with hundreds of key account managers shows that financial fluency and awareness is a major area of development. Negotiations have been witnessed where the customer's financial skills are significantly ahead of those of the key account manager. A variety of training exercises also show how difficult it is to become fluent in this key skill area.

Try these three exercises, and see how you do (no peeking at the answers!).

1 Price discount

If the trade price to your major customer is £100 per case and the gross profit is £20 per case, how much extra percentage volume do you need to keep the same cash profit if you cut the price by £2 per case?

2 Price increase

If the trade price to your major customer is £100 per case, and the gross profit is £20 per case, how much volume could you lose and still produce the same cash profit if you increased the price to £110 per case?

3 Cost of credit

A company has a turnover with an account of £1 million per annum and offers ten weeks credit at a profit margin of 5 per cent. What would the effect on margin be of a reduction of credit to eight weeks, assuming per cent interest rates?

The effect of extended credit is often dramatic, particularly when interest rates are high. An account with the same level of turnover and profit margins as the above example would produce a financial loss after four months at 15 per cent interest rate. In other words, the whole of the £50,000 margin disappears if the customer delays payment for four months or more. Again, tables can be produced that show the effects on profitability of extended credit at different interest rates.

Answers
1 Price discount

The easiest way to calculate this is to take the price cut and divide it by the new margin and percentage it:

$$\frac{2}{20-2}\% = 11.1\%$$

This means that at this margin a 2 per cent price cut requires a 11.1 per cent increase in volume to break even, i.e. to achieve the previous cash profit. This easy formula allows the key account manager to calculate price discount effects in any situation. Tables are available and the volume increases required can simply be looked up rather than calculated.

2 Price increase

You can use the same formula as Question 1,

$$\text{i.e.} \quad \frac{\text{Price increase}}{\text{New margin}}\% = \frac{10}{(20+10)}\% = 33.3\%$$

This means that you could lose one-third of your current volume sales, yet still achieve the same cash profit as before. You can prove this by using real sales volumes.

If you were currently selling 100 cases at £20 per case gross profit, you would be making £2000 gross profit. If you divide this £2000 by your new gross profit (£30) you can see that 66.66 cases (minus 33.33 per cent) will produce exactly the same cash profit.

3 Margin and credit costs

Margin of 5 per cent on £1 million = £50,000

Ten weeks' credit = approximately one-fifth of year's turnover = approximately £200,000

Interest rate of 15 per cent on this constant credit level = £30,000

Eight weeks' credit = approximately £160,000

Interest rate of 15 per cent on this credit level = £24,000

Saving = £30,000 – £24,000 = £6,000 (12 per cent of margin)

(The exact figure is a little less than £6000 because some figures have been rounded for convenient calculation.)

Summary

Account profitability information is an important tool in key account management. In general, 80 per cent of a company's sales turnover will come from 20 per cent of customers; this is the Pareto statistical distribution. It is illuminating that 80 per cent of a company's profits will also come from 20 per cent of its customers, but crucially, these are not the same 20 per cent who produce the majority of the sales. This is because the major customers can demand and obtain better prices, discounts and service levels, all of which considerably reduce the supplier's profits. Therefore the key account manager should attempt to make less profitable customers more profitable and try to grow sales turnover with those whose profitability is higher. Profit analysis has many benefits including the drawing up of a full profit and loss account which then enables comparisons to be made between major customers as well as profit improvement strategies. Financial fluency and awareness are of great importance during the ongoing negotiation process with each major customer and the key account manager themselves may be appraised and measured on profit improvement performance as part of a performance management system.

SUNDAY
MONDAY
TUESDAY
WEDNESDAY
THURSDAY
FRIDAY
SATURDAY

Fact-check (answers at the back)

1. The most important customers in terms of sales:
a) may not be the most important in terms of profit ❏
b) will definitely be the most important in terms of profit ❏
c) are the only customers worth developing ❏
d) can make significant demands of the supplier ❏

2. The Pareto statistical distribution shows that:
a) in general, 20 per cent of a company's sales turnover will come from 80 per cent of customers ❏
b) in general, 80 per cent of a company's sales turnover will come from 20 per cent of customers ❏
c) in general 50 per cent of a company's sales turnover will come from 50 per cent of customers ❏
d) per cent of sales turnover from per cent of customers varies from industry to industry ❏

3. Of a company's profits, around 80 per cent come from around 20 per cent of its customers. These are:
a) the same 20 per cent of customers who produce most of the sales ❏
b) generally not the same 20 per cent of customers who produce most of the sales ❏
c) it varies from industry to industry ❏
d) atypical results ❏

4. A supplier's profits can be considerably reduced by:
a) small customers ❏
b) promotional discounts ❏
c) reduction in prices ❏
d) service levels ❏

5. If top customers in terms of sales turnover are not also top customers in terms of profit, the key account manager should:
a) no longer deal with these customers ❏
b) try to make less profitable customers more profitable ❏
c) accept the situation ❏
d) try to grow sales turnover with customers whose profitability is higher ❏

6. Analysing the profitability of major customers is usually carried out by
a) the customer themselves ❏
b) the key account manager ❏
c) the financial department ❏
d) the customer services department ❏

7. Costs attributable to customers include:
a) key account management time ❏
b) raw materials ❏
c) promotional costs ❏
d) transport costs ❏

8. Account profitability information

a) needs to be reported to the key account manager on a regular basis ❏

b) can be reported just when convenient ❏

c) can be used as part of a performance management system ❏

d) has no value in performance management ❏

9. Profit analysis

a) facilitates comparison between major customers ❏

b) enables profit improvement strategies ❏

c) shows the current position but has no bearing on future direction ❏

d) none of the above statements are applicable ❏

10. Profit improvement strategies may include:

a) increasing sales of more profitable products ❏

b) increasing sales volume ❏

c) ending promotions ❏

d) increasing customer credit period ❏

SUNDAY

MONDAY

TUESDAY

WEDNESDAY

THURSDAY

FRIDAY

SATURDAY

WEDNESDAY

Plan for success

'If you don't know where you're going, any road will take you there.'

The key account manager must develop objectives, strategies and tactical plans to formulate a set of action priorities; to plan for success and prevent competitive threat. This plan must build on the analysis of growth opportunities and profit measurement as considered earlier to result in a final plan that is the best judgement, taking all internal and external factors into account. In the following section, the key account manager is shown how to format an account plan which takes in factors such as key facts, the SWOT analysis, customer strategy and action plan, servicing, pricing and distribution. The use of this plan in the company's own management control and information system is highlighted along with how to benchmark and report on performance. It is good practice to complete the plan to a standard format and the importance of a consistent link between objectives and performance monitoring is also explained, both of which may be facilitated by a sales plan checklist. A detailed example of such a checklist is given, with prompts for products, merchandising, promotion, servicing, pricing, distribution and communication/motivation, which relate to the headings used in the account plan format example.

Account plan format

It is best for each key account manager in a company to complete the plan to a standard format. This enables comparisons to be made between plans for different customers. It also allows the best plans to achieve the greatest resource allocation from senior management. There is no standard format for a key account plan, but an example from a fast-moving consumer goods company provides a typical set of headings in a pro forma.

1 **Key facts**
   1.1. Market sizes by product group in value, volume, market share, and growth
   1.2. Our sales by product group
   1.3. Percentage distribution levels of our key products in customer outlets
   1.4. Our profit contribution with this customer for the last two years
2 **Strengths/Weaknesses/Opportunities/Threats(SWOT analysis)**
   As per the model from Monday.
3 **Customer strategy**
   3.1 Customer appeal and our position, as shown on Monday. Summary of the customer's appeal to us (high, medium or low) and our position within the customer's business (strong, medium or weak).
   3.2. Key issues to be addressed in the planning period.
4 **Detailed customer strategy and action plan**
   4.1 **Product strategy**
      ● Product priorities for sales development
      ● Range development plans
      ● Packaging, size or feature changes planned
   4.2. **Merchandising**
      ● Product space allocation plans for customer outlets
      ● Business case propositions for increased share of customer's space
      ● Merchandising strategy for implementation by the sales force

4.3 Promotion
- Relationship to customer's advertising programme
- Timing and emphasis of promotional strategy
- Relationship of promotional investment to sales objectives
- Promotional opportunities for new store openings
- Development of unique promotional methods for this customer
- Establishment of criteria for evaluating promotional effectiveness

4.4 Servicing
- Development of service level agreements (SLAs) with different customer contact points
- Deployment of field sales force, agency staff, merchandisers and telephone sales
- Establishment of service levels in regard to warehousing, delivery, order processing, distribution and administration

4.5 Pricing
- Establishment of maximum and minimum price levels within customer outlets
- Establishment of negotiation guidelines on promotional discounts
- Agreement of maximum promotional buying periods where price discounts are applicable
- Establishment of maximum promotional discounts by product group
- Agreement of annual retrospective discount offers contingent upon sales success levels, and the establishment of negotiation parameters for the annual account plan agreement with the customer

4.6 Distribution
- Plans to increase number of customer's outlets stocking our products
- Which outlet types will produce greatest opportunities?
- Incentives to sales force for improving distribution levels
- Stock level strategies related to sales rates

4.7 Communication/Motivation/Organization

- Quality and frequency guidelines for customer communications
- Development of customer relationship management and customer newsletter policies
- Creation of customer team development and entertainment plan
- Development of trading and promotion brief to internal management/sales force/merchandisers, setting out service, activity and operating standards
- Establishment of customer contact frequencies for discussing business plans and reviewing performance
- Review of presentation quality of all communications vehicles to customer

5 Summary of customer revenue, expenditure and profit plan by product group showing the previous year and the current year's plan.

6 Promotional calendar summary showing the planned promotional events by products group for each month of the year.

The company's management control and information system will report performance against the key objectives set out in the plan on a monthly basis or more regularly, as required by the key account manager. Targets will be broken down into performance benchmarks by month, taking seasonality and promotional strategy into account.

The result is a consistent link between objectives and performance monitoring, although in many companies there is a disparity between these two. There is a great loss of effectiveness if performance targets, both quantitative and qualitative, are not reported on a consistent basis. There is a lot of truth in the sayings:

- If it's worth doing, it's worth measuring.
- What gets measured gets done.

Sales plan checklist

In order to arrive at decisions on the content of the account plan, a checklist approach should be used. The following examples are drawn from a consumer goods company servicing key accounts in the retail distribution business. The checklist headings relate to those used in the account plan format example above.

Product checklist

- Which products would we like to sell more of in this account for strategic or profit reasons?
- Where are the product growth opportunities with this customer?
- Are there gaps in the customer's range for promoting our existing products, e.g. geographically or in particular outlets? Where are these gaps, e.g. sizes, flavours, pack types, varieties?
- Are there new product opportunities for this customer, either for branded or own-label products?
- What effect will the customer's marketing strategy have on our product sales, e.g. store openings or closures, increased size of outlets, brand strategy?
- Do we need to change our product strategy, e.g. better quality, new lines, revized packaging, new sizes?

Merchandising checklist

- How are our competitors displayed in shops or depots? What share of facings do we have?
- What should we be doing to improve our share of space and impact in store or depot?
- Consider:
  - Display units
  - Promotional material
  - Sitting and traffic flow
  - Turnover and profit per square metre (what is the customer's target?)
  - Consumer handouts via merchandising teams
  - Joint activity/experiments with other suppliers
  - Shelving plans (planograms)
- How compatible is our packaging (shelf and transit)with customers' needs?
- What improvements do we need to make – quantify benefits?

Promotion checklist

- What have been or will be our objectives, for example:
  - To increase sales out – by how much?
  - To increase distribution – by how much?
  - To increase display/facings – by how much?
  - To increase customer staff motivation –measured by?
  - To increase stock levels – by how much?
- What activity was and will be planned? Include not only major promotions but also local or regional activity, special events, for example:
  - Advertising
  - New store or depot openings
  - Demonstrations
  - Incentives (include personal entertaining)
  - House magazines, public relations (PR) and competitions
  - Newsletters/bulletins/mail outs
  - Trade shows/seminars
  - Tailor-made consumer/retailer activity
- How can activity be more cost effective?
- How does our programme/investment compare with last year and competition?

Servicing checklist

- How often do we/should we make contact with head office, field management and branches?
- Who should make the contact where there is overlap? Define action responsibilities.
- What kind of selling and/or merchandising services do we/ should we provide in branches?
- How do we currently obtain and process orders?
- Could we speed up the process (obtain more allocations)? For example, telesales, automatic reordering.
- Use of computer links, e.g. Customer Relationship Management (CRM) system?
- How do we deliver product?
- How could we reduce time from obtaining order to placement of product on shelf?
- What kind of stock control objectives/systems does the customer have/employ?
- Can we assist the customer in any way to reduce out of stocks?
- What action is required by key account manager and/or our directors and others to improve relationships/influence, for example:
  - Formal marketing/business review presentations
  - Factory/head office visits
  - Involvement in customer seminars, social and sports events, celebrations, staff meetings/outings, charity sponsorship
- What services do our competitors provide? How do we compare (benchmarking standards)?
- What specialist skills and facilities could we provide as an aftersales service, for instance:
  - Staff training – product knowledge and skills
  - Merchandising

Pricing checklist

- Retail price:
  - On promotion?
  - Off promotion?
  - Compared with competition?
  - What should our discounts be?

- Discounts:
  - On promotion?
  - Off promotion?
  - How do they compare with previous year?
  - And competition?
- Customer incentive scheme for achieving annual plan:
  - Is there one?
  - Should there be one?
  - How can the present one be improved?
  - How do we compare with competition?
- Contracts:
  - Would contract pricing be an advantage?
  - How does our current or planned contract situation compare with competition?
- Could we negotiate reduced drops and/or increased drop volume, at what cost?
- Credit:
  - How long does it take us to collect due debts?
  - How can this be improved?

Distribution checklist
- Which of our products are listed by head office?
- Which of our competitors are listed by head office?
- What action needs to be taken to obtain listings? (Set a time plan)
- What are our branch or depot stock levels (weeks or months supply)?
- How do they compare with the competition, last year and trade sector average?
- How can they be increased/reduced?
- What action needs to be taken to achieve maximum distribution potential?

Communication/Motivation/Organization checklist
- How can we improve the customer's knowledge, interest and willingness to make things happen on our behalf?
- Interest and motivation can be achieved by:
  - Newsletters
  - Examples of how top staff achieved their successes

- Selling guidelines
- Use of visual aids at meetings
- League tables
- Personal letters of encouragement/thanks –customers, self, office, staff and sales force
- Organizing:
  - How activity is to be arranged
  - Who will be involved
  - What lead times are required
  - What equipment is needed
  - What skills are required
  - What training is needed
- How can organizing the customer's business be improved?

Summary

A company which prospers is one that makes things happen through good planning and the anticipation of market and competitive threats. Planning for success requires a well thought out key account plan which provides direction, objectives, strategies, action plans, budget and the benchmarks by which success may be evaluated. The plan should be written down and circulated to all those within the company who have a part to play in its implementation. At periodic review meetings the key account manager will be appraised on the delivery of the plan, with any shortfall being identified and measures taken to fill any disparity between objectives and results. Essentially the key account plan will answer three key questions: Where would we like to be? How will we get there? How will we know we are getting there? If the plans are completed to a standard format, comparisons may be made between plans for different customers and also allow for the greatest resource allocation by senior management. A consistent link between objectives and performance monitoring is paramount, with the regular reporting of targets being very effective in the assessment of this. A sales plan checklist ensures that the correct course is maintained.

SUNDAY

MONDAY

TUESDAY

WEDNESDAY

THURSDAY

FRIDAY

SATURDAY

Fact-check (answers at the back)

1. Planning for success aims to develop objectives, strategies and tactical plans to:
a) give the key account manager a set of action priorities ❑
b) prevent competitive threat ❑
c) form the basis of successful evaluation ❑
d) avoid the need for further negotiation ❑

2. It is good practice for each key account manager in a company to complete the account plan to a standard format. This:
a) enables comparisons to be made between plans for different customers ❑
b) does not enable comparisons between plans for different customers ❑
c) allows the best plans to achieve the greatest resource allocation ❑
d) has no influence on resource allocation ❑

3. Performance targets are effective if reported on a consistent basis. Which of the following statements are applicable?
a) only quantitative targets are relevant ❑
b) only qualitative targets are relevant ❑
c) both qualitative and quantitative targets are relevant ❑
d) sales figures alone are relevant to performance targets ❑

4. A key account plan builds on the analysis of growth opportunities and the measurement of profits by account. Which of the following statements is also true?
a) the best plan is the first and most obvious outcome ❑
b) a series of alternative strategies and actions will be generated ❑
c) the final plan will be the best judgement taking internal and external factors into account ❑
d) the plan should be circulated to all within the company who have a part to play in its implementation ❑

5. At periodic review meetings, the key account manager will be appraised on delivery of the plan according to criteria of
a) content and quality ❑
b) timing ❑
c) budget ❑
d) simplicity ❑

6. Which three of the following questions are relevant to the key account plan?
a) where are we now? ❑
b) where would we like to be? ❑
c) how will we get there? ❑
d) how will we know we're getting there? ❑

65

7. In assessing customer strategy in the account plan format, which of the following should be taken into account?
a) customer appeal, whether high, medium or low ❏
b) any potential customer has appeal, irrespective of their position ❏
c) our position within the customer's business, whether strong, medium or weak ❏
d) our present position is irrelevant; where we aim to be is all that matters ❏

8. With regard to the merchandising checklist for a sales plan:
a) the displays of competitors are not relevant ❏
b) the displays of competitors are relevant ❏
c) consideration should be given to the compatibility of packaging with customers' needs ❏
d) it is not necessary to accommodate customers' needs in the design of packaging ❏

9. The pricing checklist of a sales plan should consider
a) trying to get away with the highest price possible, even if it is unsustainable ❏
b) retail price ❏
c) discounts ❏
d) customer incentive scheme ❏

10. Companies which prosper
a) make up a plan as they go along ❏
b) achieve results through good planning ❏
c) measure and evaluate success ❏
d) anticipate market and competitive threats ❏

SUNDAY

MONDAY

TUESDAY

WEDNESDAY

THURSDAY

FRIDAY

SATURDAY

THURSDAY

Negotiate to win-win

In the ongoing relationship between key account manager and customer there is a significant element of negotiation, which can occur during any stage of the business. A successful key account manager must understand the difference between negotiation and selling, plan effectively in advance of the negotiation and be able to conduct negotiations to produce a win-win situation. These secrets will soon be revealed. Negotiation versus selling depends on whether the need to supply is equal to or exceeds the need to buy. In planning to negotiate there are five steps which the key account manager should follow. In the following pages the account manager will see that they need to look at the situation from the customer's viewpoint as well as from their own. Both sides have objectives that must be considered and met, forming a list of negotiation variables, often called the 'shopping list'; some examples are given. Guidelines for conducting negotiations are also set out along with the core principles of negotiation which must be learned. The realization of relative strengths and weaknesses is a great skill in negotiation, which is always a high pressure situation owing to the significant costs and values to be maintained.

Negotiation versus selling

Selling occurs when the need to supply exceeds the need to buy. It involves persuading the buyer that the supplier's products are needed.

Negotiation assumes that the need to supply is equal to the need to buy – it is the give and take process whereby the conditions and terms of a transaction or relationship are agreed.

Key account managers still have to use their selling skills to develop relationships with their accounts and to put forward their case, yet negotiation is more prominent in maintaining business. The following chart illustrates this point.

Selling versus negotiation

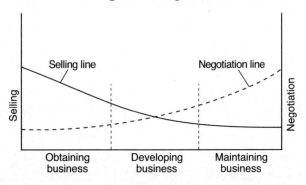

Planning to negotiate

Before every negotiation, the key account manager should follow five steps:

Planning stages

1 Assess buyer needs/identify areas for negotiation
2 Cost/benefit analysis
3 Assess stances that buyer will take

4 Relate to your objectives
5 Plan your own stances

Assess buyer needs

- What are the buyer's commercial needs?
- What will be the effect of purchase or no purchase?
- What problems does the customer have?
- What alternatives exist, e.g. competitive offers?
- What subjective needs exist, e.g. security, status, peace of mind?
- What is the relative importance of each need?
- What 'shopping list' of negotiable areas will the buyer raise?

The purpose of this stage is to enable the key account manager to look at the situation from the customer's viewpoint. This is the skill of empathy and research shows that successful negotiators are particularly strong in putting themselves in the customer's shoes.

You need to prepare a number of questions in advance which aim to identify the key issues in the customer's buying situation. You also have to anticipate the needs of different interests within the customer's organization structure. As an example, the buyer may invite the marketing director to attend a meeting and perhaps the distribution manager. These three job roles will have a different emphasis for each need.

Cost/benefit analysis

- What concessions can you offer?
- What concessions will you seek from the buyer?
- What are the costs and benefits of these concessions?
- What concessions cost us little, but are of considerable value to the buyer?

For the key account manager, the aim of this planning is to prepare costs and values in advance of the meeting to ensure that you are not caught out. It is much better to come to the meeting prepared, than to admit that you do not know a figure and have to refer to head office.

Even worse, if you are not prepared financially, you may give away an important financial concession without getting anything worthwhile in return. Skilled buyers are able to exert psychological pressure to get an agreement and it is easy to miss an opportunity.

It is best to make concessions that do not have a simple cash cost. For instance, if you think the buyer will ask for an extra cash discount, you can plan to offer extra support services (e.g. training), which will be of benefit to the buyer but cost you nothing in real financial outlay. This could happen if you had spare capacity in your training department, which could provide training for your customer at no immediate extra cash cost for your company.

Assess stances that buyer will take

- What is the real strength of the buyer's need?
- How will the buyer state this in the extreme stance?
- What will be done to pull you towards this position?
- What will the buyer's real stance be?

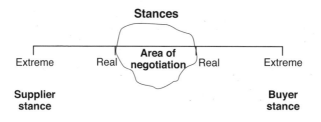

Stances

Area of negotiation

Extreme — Real — Area of negotiation — Real — Extreme

Supplier stance | **Buyer stance**

In the diagram, both the buyer and supplier may begin the meeting with extreme positions designed to throw the other side off their position. Two examples demonstrate the importance of this type of negotiation planning.

The first example is an annual contract negotiation, where two key account managers meet two buyers. The first action of one of the buyers was to tear up a previously submitted proposal from the supplier and state, 'If this is the best you can do, there is no basis for any agreement, and we will have to review your competitive position with us.' Fortunately, one of the key account managers recognized this is a ritual initial ploy, and defused the situation by making a joke. This lightened the atmosphere and the negotiation proceeded in an amicable manner.

The second example is of a key account manager replacing a previously successful manager. The first gesture of the buyer was to hand over a long list of items which he said he would no longer stock unless the supplier offered the same terms given to another key account. The buyer had found out through the grapevine that another customer was getting better terms from the supplier.

In this case, the extreme stance completely caught the key account manager unawares, and she had no arguments pre-prepared. The effect was that she had to call off the meeting and refer to head office, thus giving the buyer a significant psychological edge.

Relate to your objectives

- What do you need to achieve?
- What conflict exists with the buyer's needs?
- What common ground exists?
- How can differences be resolved by negotiation?
- How can the buyer's objectives be achieved together with yours?

The key issue is to know the 'walk away' point. This is a set point of cost concessions in relation to benefits you receive, which you cannot go below.

In role-play practice sessions with key account managers, it is amazing how many times too much is given away by the supplier under pressure to retain business with the customer. Every negotiation has a price and the rewards for good preparation at this stage are evident in more profitable deals.

Plan your own stances

- What bargaining point do you have?
- How can you raise value relative to cost?
- How will you match concessions on each side?
- What stances will you open with?
- What are your real stances?
- Who will be involved in the negotiation?

The key account manager can plan to negotiate from a significant list of negotiation variables, often called the 'shopping list'. With enough preparation, the buyer's shopping list can be anticipated and creative trading of concessions can take place within the overall negotiation framework.

Examples of negotiable variables

1 Schedules of production/delivery
2 Cost
3 Training
4 Maintenance contracts
5 Flexible working hours
6 Performance standards
7 Sale or return
8 Long-term contracts
9 Allowance for exhibitions/display
10 Use of staff
11 Delivery dates/locations
12 Tailoring of solutions/materials (e.g. packaging)
13 Storage costs
14 Support packages
15 Enhancements
16 Penalties for non-performance
17 Installation and implementation support
18 Stock holding levels
19 Discounts/incentives/bonuses
20 Promotional support
21 Exclusivity
22 Deferred price increase
23 Cash flow/payment terms
24 Use of machine/machine time for development
25 Fixed or variable prices
26 Investment money
27 Type of materials used
28 Leasing or outright sale
29 Complexity of solution
30 Speed of delivery
31 Guarantees/indemnities
32 Samples/free product
33 Joint advertising/branding

34 Future commitment for further work
35 Notice periods
36 Experience/specialist skills provision
37 Use of premises
38 Backup (hardware, staff)
39 Call-out terms (rates, time)
40 Expense rates
41 Documentation provision (e.g. reports)
42 Charge for secretarial support

Conducting negotiations

1 Let the buyer talk first, so that you know the full shopping list
2 Establish real stances without buyer 'losing face', moving from extreme stances
3 Avoid premature deadlock – be flexible
4 Trial close frequently – 'If we did this, would you do that . . .?'
5 Trade concessions one at a time – 'I'll agree, if you will . . .'
6 Add value to your concessions – 'We have never done this before . . .'
7 Devalue buyer's concessions – 'That is available to us anyway . . .'
8 Get commitment regularly – 'So let us agree what we have accepted . . .'
9 Be confident – assertive, unemotional, friendly
10 Maintain 'social fabric' – negotiation is a ritual game for real stakes
11 Ensure buyer gets the satisfaction needed, both objective and subjective – you both need to 'win'

The skilful negotiator begins by obtaining the buyer's shopping list right at the start. It is easy to be drawn into making further concessions if your first offer is not acceptable, unless you ask the customer for their requirements first.

The greatest skill in conducting negotiations is to realize your relative strengths and weaknesses. You can then trade concessions creatively within an overall shopping list structure.

The selling skill of persuasion should be used to help you to secure the best deal possible, relative to the situation you face. Like two poker players, sometimes you will have good cards and can speak from strength, but sometimes you have a poor hand and must use bluffing tactics to help your position.

The core principles of negotiation can be summarized as follows:

Negotiation principles

Some dos
- Show respect
- Be patient
- Confess limits to authority
- Communicate well

- Trade concessions
- Rehearse/prepare
- Respect confidences
- End positively

Some don'ts
- Show emotion
- Confront
- Betray confidential information
- Compromise minimum objectives
- Relax guard
- Underestimate
- Dominate
- Irritate

The key account manager can PASS the test by:

Planning effectively for the likely areas of the negotiation, the costs of concessions and the likely trading areas.

Asserting themselves during the meeting, but being flexible enough to achieve a compromise.

Searching for variables which can be traded creatively during the give and take process.

Summarizing the points of agreement during the negotiations and summarizing actions to be taken to resolve any matters not yet agreed.

The habits of negotiation can be taken to extremes. In the 19th century, a Foreign Minister was negotiating with his counterpart of another country. During the lengthy negotiation process, this Foreign Minister died. On being given the news, his counterpart replied 'I wonder what he meant by that?'

Summary

The ability to negotiate is a core skill for key account managers and can be developed through practice and training. The aim is to achieve a win-win situation in a challenging but friendly atmosphere. Key account managers must still use their selling skills to develop relationships with their accounts and to put forward their case, yet negotiation is more prominent in maintaining business. All negotiation should be planned, following five steps: identifying areas for negotiation, undertaking a cost/benefit analysis, assessing the stances the buyer will take, relating to the key account manager's own objectives and planning their own stance. Having planned the negotiation, the key account manager must consider the situation from the customer's viewpoint; successful negotiators are particularly strong in empathizing with their customer. There is a significant list of negotiation variables and the skilful negotiator begins by obtaining the buyer's shopping list right at the start. Concessions can then be traded creatively, with the selling skill of persuasion being used to help secure the best deal possible, adhering to the do's and don'ts of negotiation principles. Finally, summarize the points of agreement during the negotiations as well as the actions to be taken to resolve any matters not yet agreed.

SUNDAY
MONDAY
TUESDAY
WEDNESDAY
THURSDAY
FRIDAY
SATURDAY

Fact-check (answers at the back)

1. Negotiation can occur:
a) only at the start of the relationship with the customer ❏
b) during any stage of the relationship ❏
c) where an annual contract needs to be agreed ❏
d) where individual transactions form part of the relationship ❏

2. Select the correct statements. Negotiation:
a) is not the same as selling ❏
b) is the same as selling ❏
c) is a give and take process ❏
d) has an outright winner and a clear loser ❏

3. Select the correct statements. Selling:
a) assumes that the need to supply is equal to the need to buy ❏
b) occurs when the need to supply outstrips the need to buy ❏
c) involves persuading the buyer that the supplier's products are needed ❏
d) is a skill not required in negotiation ❏

4. When planning to negotiate, how many stages are there to follow?
a) one ❏
b) five ❏
c) ten ❏
d) it varies from time to time ❏

5. When planning to negotiate:
a) the key account manager must look at the situation from the customer's viewpoint ❏
b) the key account manager needs only to consider their own viewpoint; the customer can look after themselves ❏
c) successful negotiators avoid empathizing with the customer so as not to be distracted from their aims ❏
d) successful negotiators are particularly strong at putting themselves in their customer's shoes. ❏

6. During the negotiations:
a) it is always possible to strike a deal ❏
b) there is a 'walk away' point ❏
c) there is a creative trading of concessions ❏
d) the atmosphere is unlikely to be pressured or hostile ❏

7. There is usually a significant list of negotiation variables, often called
a) the wish list ❏
b) the to-do list ❏
c) the dream list ❏
d) the shopping list ❏

8. A skilful negotiator:
a) makes their own requirements known first to dominate the negotiation ❏
b) lets the buyer talk first to learn the full shopping list ❏
c) seeks to diminish the buyer's confidence to be able to achieve their own goals ❏
d) ensures the buyer gets satisfaction also – you both need to 'win' ❏

9. Which of the following are good principles of negotiation:
a) showing emotion ❏
b) confessing limits to authority ❏
c) showing respect ❏
d) relaxing one's guard ❏

10. Which of the following statements are applicable to negotiation:
a) skills of negotiation can be developed through continuous practice and training ❏
b) there are significant costs and values to be obtained on both sides ❏
c) the aim is to achieve a good compromise ❏
d) none of the above ❏

FRIDAY

Control activity levels

Activity levels and standards of performance must be monitored by the key account manager to enable the presentation of plans and progress to customers and to measure success against these plans. In the following section the importance of information management is explained as this is crucial to the control cycle. It will be seen that objectives are the absolute success measures, covering the quantifiable goals. The key results areas are the means by which objectives are achieved and include all the activity levels necessary to service the account; these activity levels are a key part of the planning and control process but judging the relationship between activity levels and success can be challenging. Once the key results areas are established, standards of performance, both qualitative and quantitative, can be set for each type of activity with major customers. The collection and analysis of results by the key account manager enables performance to be measured against all set standards and requires the formation of a key account information system. If standards are not being achieved, diagnosis and corrective action must be implemented; suggestions and examples for both of these are given.

The control cycle is shown below:

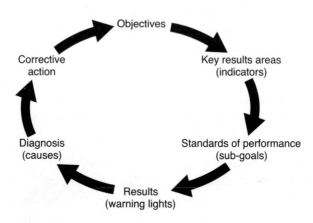

Managing with information

1 Objectives

These are the absolute success measures and will cover the quantifiable goals such as sales, turnover and volume, profit and market share of the customer's business.

2 Key results areas

These are the means by which objectives are achieved and include all the activity levels necessary to service the account, as specified by the key account manager.

These activity levels are a key part of the planning and control process because they answer the question, 'What causes success?' Many people will contribute to these activity levels. Examples include:

● Sales force call frequencies, necessary to service the account
● Amount and quality of time spent with the customer
● Administrative contacts with the customer's administrative department

- Senior management contacts with the customer's equivalent levels of management
- Marketing department contacts with the customer's marketing department
- Operational service levels in areas such as manufacturing, warehousing and transport
- Telephone and e-mail contact levels
- Financial and credit control activity levels

It is an art, rather than a science, to judge the relationship between activity levels and success. The supplier has limited resources of people and time available to contact each major customer and the customer has limited resources to respond to each supplier. Previous experience is the best guide to establishing what activity levels are required, and it is important to keep reviewing both the frequency and quality of all contact levels with major customers.

3 Standards of performance

Once the key results areas are established, standards of performance can be set for each type of activity with major customers. These can be either quantitative or qualitative.

Quantitative standards would cover areas such as:

- Number of calls to be made by sales force
- Time spent per call
- Frequency of business reviews with customer
- Credit control payment standards

These standards can be set and agreed with each member of the team who has contact with the major customer. In some cases, a key account manager will set measurable activity standards for hundreds of company staff who have either direct or indirect contact with that major customer. If the supplier has a significant number of major customers, there will be an intricate jigsaw of measurable performance standards, which will establish activity levels for a large proportion of the total staff.

Qualitative Standards define the quality levels of these activities.

- Once call frequencies are established for the sales force, the qualitative standards will define what is achieved during each call. For example, the salesperson may be required to follow a standard process for each visit, which may include checking stock levels, ensuring products are displayed or used correctly, agreeing service standards with customer staff, etc.
- Administrative staff may have quantitative standards for their response times to queries or times taken to answer telephones, but there may be important qualitative standards to set for the way that responses are handled and the quality of service given to the customer. Quality of customer contact may be more important than the number of contacts made, so both should be measured.
- The presentation of the annual account plan to each major customer is a quantitative standard, but the way it is presented is qualitative. Each company should develop a format tailored to its own market, but the following is an example drawn from a consumer goods company supplying retail distributors.

Annual account plan presentation

Stage 1	**Review last year's trading performance** ● Volume/sterling turnover ● Expenditure budget ● Promotion programme ● Marketing support ● Range stocked, gains/losses ● Distribution levels by product
Stage 2	**New year's objective/strategy** ● Set turnover target/earnings target ● Promotion strategy ● Distribution/listings objectives ● Marketing plans, etc.
Stage 3	**Incentive discount scheme** ● Outline earnings achieved ● Present new proposition
Stage 4	**Account plans** ● Store opening/closing programme ● Promotions programme ● Stocking policy ● Pricing policy, etc.

Stage 5	**Justification of account plans** Sales increases due to: ● Inflation ● Store maturity (sales increases due to new stores becoming fully operational) ● New store openings ● Brand maturity (sales increases due to new brands becoming fully accepted and distributed) ● Promotional support ● Market growth ● Market share growth ● New listings ● New products ● Shelf space/relays
	Sales decreases due to: ● Store closures ● Brand deletions

● In reviewing performance with the major customer, quarterly reviews are a quantified standard of performance (they could be more or less frequent). How these reviews are carried out are qualitative standards. Again, each company is different, but the quarterly review format for the same company as above, would be as follows:

Quarterly reviews

Stage 1	**Review trading situation** ● Versus same period last year ● Versus incentive discount scheme (including targets to pull back any deficit) ● Versus objective set with account
Stage 2	**Review promotional programme** ● Result of promotions already run ● Reconfirm remainder of programme ● Discuss any changes re. Stage 1 results
Stage 3	**Review marketing support** ● Results of activity already run ● Reconfirm rest of year ● Present any changes to plans
Stage 4	**Accounts plans** ● Identify any changes to policy that will affect your plans

Each qualitative standard of performance forms the basis of a performance management system for all members of staff who have a role to play in servicing major customers. To assist in performance management, different levels can be established, for instance:

● Below standard
● Meets standard
● Above standard
● Exceptional

These standards can form the basis of coaching at all levels on the job, and for developing off the job training programmes.

4 Results

The key account manager needs to collect and analyse results so that performance can be measured against all set standards. This requires the formation of a key account information system.

Setting up any sort of key customer information system is complex and can be expensive because it requires information to be collected by the customer rather than by traditional accounting categories. Both quantitative and qualitative information may be difficult to collect and some staff may not wish to accurately record all their activities. Computerization has made quantitative results reporting more precise, but reporting on qualitative standards is always difficult. The fact that it may be difficult should not mean that it is not done at all.

Various types of documentation will require development and continual modification to ensure their accuracy. These documents could include call reports, service standard reports, customer surveys, account information records, etc. Each information system will be tailored to individual companies and there can be no standard specification.

If results, both quantitative and qualitative, are measured against standards, variances against each standard can be managed by the key account manager. If standards are not being achieved, the next two stages of the control process must be implemented – diagnosis and corrective action.

5 Diagnosis

The key account manager has to motivate the line managers of those teams of staff where there is performance shortfall.

Diagnosis aims to identify when results are not being met due to a fall in quantitative standards (e.g. the sales force is not calling often enough or spending enough time on key accounts) or where there are qualitative shortfalls in standards. A fall in qualitative standards requires a diagnosis of possible causes. The following are examples:

- Declining motivation
- Lack of training (attitude, skill or knowledge)
- Poor planning
- Lack of promotional effort
- Poor organization
- Need for incentives
- Recruitment failures

These causes can often only be identified from personal meetings and discussion with the staff members concerned. Investigation may often reveal some complex behavioural or cultural issues.

6 Corrective action

Once the problems have been diagnosed, the key account manager can help to influence corrective action. This may involve discussions with other line managers or assisting with developing training programme specifications. Corrective actions may entail:

- Improved activity management
- Better/more frequent coaching
- Revised training programmes
- Better staff management methods
- New control and measurement systems

Experience shows that improving quality in managing major customers is a process of constant improvement and continual activity management. The key account manager rarely has responsibility for other members of staff within the company. Thus, there is a need to develop influencing skills so that other managers and their staff can be motivated to deliver the right quality of service to each major customer.

Apart from taking corrective action involving people issues, which are often outside the key account manager's direct control, there will be many times when performance falls below set objectives and corrective action needs to be taken.

For example, if a major customer is falling short of the profit objectives set for it, corrective action could involve an appraisal of the following alternatives:

- Increasing price levels
- Reducing discounts
- Redirecting effort to higher margin product lines
- Increasing volume by cost effective promotional methods
- Reducing account servicing costs
- Negotiating new contract terms
- Reducing financial costs to customer

Each of these alternatives will require detailed appraisal and there may be no easy solutions because the customer could resist the revised action plan.

Summary

A good plan must be measured and managed for it to become a successful plan and the control of activity levels for each major customer is an essential task for the key account manager. The objectives are the absolute success measures and cover quantifiable goals such as sales, turnover and volume, profit and market share of the customer's business. The key results areas are the means by which the objectives are achieved and include all the activity levels necessary to service the account. Judging the relationship between activity levels and success is an art, so previous experience is the best guide to establishing the required levels of activity. Once the key results are established, standards of performance can be set for each type of activity with major customers; both quantitative, such as number of calls made and time spent per call and qualitative, such as the way responses are handled and the standard of the service given. The key account manager needs to collect and analyse results so that performance can be measured against all set standards. Diagnosis to identify when results are not being met due to qualitative or quantitative shortfalls in standards allows corrective action to be applied.

Fact-check (answers at the back)

1. In controlling activity levels, select which of the following statements apply:
   a) the key account manager needs to present plans and progress to customers ❏
   b) the key account manager does not need to present plans and progress to customers ❏
   c) success must be measured against plans through standards of performance ❏
   d) success does not need to be measured; this has no benefit. ❏

2. Objectives are the absolute success measures and cover quantifiable goals such as:
   a) sales ❏
   b) turnover and volume ❏
   c) customer satisfaction ❏
   d) profit and market share of the customer's business ❏

3. Staff relevant to the activity levels servicing the account include
   a) the key account manager only ❏
   b) the customer services team only ❏
   c) the senior management contacts with customer's equivalent levels of management ❏
   d) all staff who are involved in servicing the account ❏

4. When considering the relationship between activity levels and success
   a) the relationship may be judged scientifically ❏
   b) it is a subjective judgement ❏
   c) there is no guide to the required levels of activity ❏
   d) previous experience is the best guide to establishing activity levels ❏

5. Standards of performance may be:
   a) quantitative only ❏
   b) qualitative only ❏
   c) either qualitative or quantitative ❏
   d) set and agreed with each member of the team in contact with the customer ❏

6. How many stages are there in the annual account plan presentation?
   a) one ❏
   b) three ❏
   c) five ❏
   d) ten ❏

7. The collection and analysis of results involves several challenges. Which of the following statements is true?
a) if the information is difficult or expensive to collect, the costs outweigh the benefits so it should not be done ❑
b) documentation only needs an initial set-up and will then be relevant for the duration of the relationship ❑
c) development and continual modification of documentation will ensure accuracy ❑
d) it is not necessary to tailor the system to individual companies ❑

8. Diagnosis aims to identify when results are not being met. This may be:
a) due to a fall in quantitative standards ❑
b) due to a fall in qualitative standards ❑
c) identified from personal meetings and discussion with staff ❑
d) unrelated to the above possibilities ❑

9. Corrective actions may entail:
a) improved activity management ❑
b) changing the objectives to make them easier to achieve ❑
c) revised training programmes ❑
d) new control and measurement systems ❑

10. If a major customer is falling short of the profit objectives set for it, corrective action could involve:
a) increasing price levels ❑
b) reducing discounts ❑
c) redirecting effort to higher margin profit lines ❑
d) an easy solution, as the customer is likely to welcome negotiating new terms ❑

SUNDAY

MONDAY

TUESDAY

WEDNESDAY

THURSDAY

FRIDAY

SATURDAY

SATURDAY

Manage relationships

In this final section the key account manager is introduced to the Relational Model which describes how the key account relationship changes as it moves from a transactional focus (short-term sales achievement) to collaboration (long-term customer value and retention). The relationship with the customer must be managed and the five stages of key account management in the development of this relationship are introduced. These stages may be broken down as pre, early, mid, partnership and synergistic key account management. The characteristics of these stages are fully explained. There is also a sixth stage to be considered, which is what occurs when the relationship with the customer has broken down; uncoupling. Factors which may cause uncoupling are listed. Purchasing management trends that favour the development of relationship suppliers are also considered as these have become more relevant in recent years and can have a significant influence. The SCOPE model of successful partnerships is also introduced, encompassing strategic factors, cultural and chemistry factors, organizational and operational factors, performance review and reporting factors as well as equality factors. In summary, a comparison is made between transactional and relationship key account management.

Relational model

There is an increasing importance in key account management to build relationships by linking supplier company staff more closely with major customer staff. There is a move away from a transactional focus (short-term sales achievement) to a relationship focus (long-term customer value and retention).

This trend in relationships development has been accurately analysed by Tony Millman and Kevin Wilson in the key account Relational Model. This describes how the key account relationship changes as it moves from transactions to collaboration.

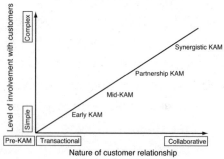

Key account relational model

KAM= Key account management

Source: *Key Customers: how to manage them profitably*

Malcolm McDonald, Butterworth-Heinemann, 2000. Based on the work of Millman and Wilson.

The five stages of key account management (KAM) development are characterized by Millman and Wilson and supported by further research from Malcolm McDonald and Beth Rogers:

1 Pre-KAM

● Identify potential key accounts
● Establish the first customer needs
● Seek initial entry points

2 Early KAM

- Initial transactions established
- Small share of customer's business
- Key account manager/purchasing manager relationship
- Aim to understand customer's decision making unit

3 Mid KAM

- Selling company is a preferred supplier
- Interactions increase in numbers and complexity
- Trust levels increase
- Contact levels increase to involve directors, other managers, specialists and operational staff
- Wariness on both sides about 'putting too many eggs in one basket'

4 Partnership KAM

- Supply and share of customer's business may approach 100 per cent
- Development of partnership agreements
- Growth of team working to improve quality and reduce costs in both companies
- Sharing of sensitive information
- Long-term pricing and product development policies
- Open book financial information shared
- Shared expertise at all levels
- All departments at each company fully aligned

5 Synergistic KAM

- A 'beyond partnership' stage
- A single entity, rather than two organizations
- Joint value (synergy) created at all levels
- Exit barriers on either side are high
- Joint planning at all levels

SUNDAY MONDAY TUESDAY WEDNESDAY THURSDAY FRIDAY SATURDAY

- Cross-functional focus teams work on joint business improvement projects
- Key account relationships may cut across country lines and become global

Uncoupling KAM

There is a sixth stage not presented in this analysis, and that is uncoupling key account management. This describes a breaking down of the relationship and it can occur at any of the five stages described. It may be caused by factors such as:

- Changes in key personnel
- Change in corporate buying policy, for example, a retailer may decide to source its purchases on a global basis rather than in its home market
- Breakdown of trust, for instance, a failure to communicate a product quality problem or preferred buying terms given to a competitor of the major customer
- Complacency
- Cultural factors – where there is a mismatch between a bureaucratic supplier and an entrepreneurial customer
- Quality, for example, if either company suffers a serious decline in product, process or people quality
- Declining market position – where either company suffers a significant loss of market share
- Financial problems – if either party suffers significant financial problems

Trends favouring relationships

In recent years, there have been a variety of purchasing management trends that favour the development of relationships with suppliers. These trends include:

- Centralization of buying
- Global sourcing of supplies
- Just-in-time (JIT) inventory management systems
- Zero defects quality management
- Outsourcing of supplies

- Focus on total supply chain management
- Computerized techniques for materials management and routine transactions
- Development of preferred supplier buying processes
- Increased size and scale of purchasing due to mergers and acquisitions

Taking one example from the above list, the just-in-time delivery systems are based on the Japanese high dependency theory. This tries to eliminate waste by getting everyone involved, including key suppliers. The result is a joint continuous improvement process known as KAIZEN.

One piece of recent research showed that Japanese auto component companies supply 24 times the value per vehicle compared with USA companies in the same market. Japanese manufacturers bought twice the volume of components from one-tenth of the number of suppliers, compared with USA companies.

This favours the development of what the consultancy Bain & Co. calls Value Managed Relationships. These are collaborative partnerships aimed at retaining major customers, and key account managers play a major role as the interface in this relationship building process.

Some research carried out by Roger Pudney of Ashridge Management College has identified the following competitive advantages from partnerships, which are relevant to the development of more advanced key account management relationships.

Competitive advantages from partnership

- Strategic long-term developments
- Higher margins/higher prices
- Volume increases
- Easier negotiations
- Economies of scale/manufacturing efficiencies
- Reduced delivery times
- Blocking competitors
- Early problem solving

- Early information
- Faster new products
- Security of supply

The Ashridge research developed an easy to remember SCOPE model of successful partnerships:

Strategic factors include shared vision and strategy, making long-term commitments and a significant investment in the partnership, ensuring that the partners' strengths are complementary.

Cultural and chemistry factors include managing the fit between the two cultures and building strong personal relationships.

Organizational and operational factors principally find ways to integrate and link the partners together at many levels.

Performance review and reporting factors include setting up a regular mutual evaluation system to assess the effectiveness of the partnership.

Equality factors are mainly softer behavioural factors, such as building mutual trust and treating each other as equals.

Successful partnerships
SCOPE model

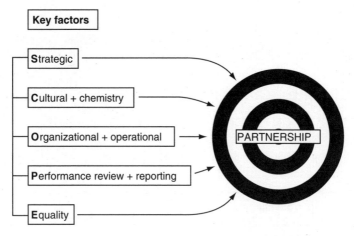

Souce: R. Pudney Ashridge International Partnership Study

The type of relationship between supplier and customer will determine the qualities the key account manager needs to develop. Some major customers will not require their relationships with key account managers to venture beyond the management of the sales transaction processes. Other customers favour a more sophisticated relationship moving towards partnership and that will require a different type of key account manager.

These differences are shown below:

Transactional key account management	Relationship key account management
Sales focus	Customer retention focus
Simple negotiations	Complex negotiations
Competitive threats	Limited or no competition
Supply of products/services	Joint creation of products/services
Short time-scale	Long time-scale
Limited range of contacts	Extensive range of contacts
Low service levels	High service levels
Cost/price focus	Value focus
Adversarial	Partnership
Occasional communication	Frequent communication
Some cooperation	Total cooperation

China's Chairman Mao Tse Tung, once famously quoted 'A journey of a thousand miles begins with a single step.' A week is the first step in a journey and we wish you the very best of luck in reaching your destination.

Summary

The move from short-term sales achievement to collaboration, with long-term customer value and retention, means it is increasingly important in key account management to build relationships by linking supplier company staff more closely with major customer staff. This trend is shown by the Relational Model. The different stages of the relationship have different characteristics, from seeking initial entry points (pre-KAM) to winning a small share of the customer's business (early-KAM), to becoming a preferred supplier (mid-KAM) through to partnership and beyond. As these stages progress the customer and the key account manager become increasingly aligned and interdependent; there are many competitive advantages from partnership. Trends such as centralization of buying and global sourcing of supplies favour the development of relationships with suppliers and there is a SCOPE model of successful partnerships. The qualities a key account manager needs to possess are determined by the type of relationship between supplier and customer. Excellent sales skills will be appropriate for early KAM and perhaps mid KAM, but the ability to manage complex customer relationships is also essential if the relationship is to become less transactional.

SUNDAY
MONDAY
TUESDAY
WEDNESDAY
THURSDAY
FRIDAY
SATURDAY

Fact-check (answers at the back)

1. The description of how the key account relationship changes as it moves from transactions to collaboration is called the Relational:
   a) Progress ❏
   b) Model ❏
   c) Development ❏
   d) Change ❏

2. Which of the following statements apply to the developing relationship with customers in key account management?
   a) the level of involvement moves from simple from complex ❏
   b) the level of involvement is complex to begin with then becomes simple ❏
   c) the nature of the relationship moves from transactional to collaborative ❏
   d) the nature of the relationship moves from collaborative to transactional ❏

3. How many stages are there of key account management?
   a) one ❏
   b) five ❏
   c) ten ❏
   d) an infinite number ❏

4. Which of the following statements is applicable to Partnership KAM?
   a) supply and share of customer's business may approach 100 per cent ❏
   b) supplier and customer introduce new levels of confidentiality ❏
   c) sensitive information is shared ❏
   d) financial information is closely guarded ❏

5. Which of the following statements is applicable to Synergistic KAM?
   a) it is always easy to end the synergism ❏
   b) exit barriers on either side are high ❏
   c) the two companies remain distinct ❏
   d) there is a single entity, rather than two organizations ❏

6. Uncoupling KAM is the phrase used to describe a breaking down of the business relationship. Which of the following may be a cause of uncoupling?
   a) changes in key personnel ❏
   b) an improvement in product, process or people quality ❏
   c) complacency ❏
   d) financial problems ❏

7. A value managed relationship is one which
a) is entirely dependent on the value of the sales ❏
b) sees the key account manager having a low profile in the relationship ❏
c) is a collaborative partnership aimed at retaining major customers ❏
d) is one whereby the supplier charges the customer for every service delivered ❏

8. Which of the following are competitive advantages from partnerships?
a) higher margins/higher prices ❏
b) security of supply ❏
c) blocking competitors ❏
d) none of the above ❏

9. The Ashridge research developed an easy to remember model of successful partnership called:
a) RANGE ❏
b) REACH ❏
c) EXTENT ❏
d) SCOPE ❏

10. In a comparison between transactional and relationship key account management, which of the following statements is true?
a) transactional KAM focuses on sales ❏
b) relationship KAM has low service levels ❏
c) relationship KAM is adversarial ❏
d) transactional KAM is short time-scale ❏

SUNDAY

MONDAY

TUESDAY

WEDNESDAY

THURSDAY

FRIDAY

SATURDAY

7 × 7

1 Seven key ideas

- Work harder at knowing your customer. Understanding your customer, through better knowledge of them and their market, is vitally important when profits are being squeezed.

- Ensure your internal customer information management system is up to date. This will help you to assess your growth opportunities and help you in your negotiations with key customers.

- Promote value-added services to customers, to give you a competitive edge, and reduce the focus on price and cost.

- Develop better working and personal relationships with customers, to develop more empathy with them and to understand their key issues and possible solutions.

- Build up your internal team in terms of better relationships, communication and motivation – managing major customers is always a team effort.

- Continually update your assessments of customer and market segment profitability, as opportunities always exist for reducing costs or creating extra value. Sales growth at a loss is not a good strategy in the long term.

- Keep sight of the future. Tough times do not last forever, and you need to capitalize on new opportunities and market changes when they happen.

2 Seven best resources

- www.keyaccountmanagement.org This is a global resource to share knowledge and learning on key account management.

- www.strategicaccounts.org SAMA is a non-profit association aimed at helping establish key account management as a separate profession and at developing a corporate strategy for growth.

- www.som.cranfield.ac.uk Cranfield Business School is a major specialist in key account management, and this site is a club for best practice sharing of ideas.

- *Key Account Management: The Definitive Guide* by Malcolm McDonald and Diana Woodburn (Butterworth Heinemann, 2011). This book offers state-of-the-art strategies in tools and processes.

- *Relationship Management for Competitive Advantage* by Adrian Payne, Martin Christopher, Moira Clark and Helen Peck (Butterworth Heinemann, 1998). This has some excellent writing from around the world.

- *From Key Account Selling to Key Account Management*, Tony Millman and Kevin Wilson, Tenth Annual Conference on Industrial Marketing and Purchasing (1994). This introduced the pioneering key account relational development model (see Saturday chapter).

- *Major Account Sales Strategy* by Neil Rackham (McGraw Hill, 1989). The author of *SPIN Selling* wrote this book to focus on the creative sales aspects of key account management.

3 Seven things to avoid

- Focusing on internal matters instead of the customer.
- Becoming complacent in your processes and systems of customer management.
- Forgetting that profit is more important to the company than sales.
- Delaying personal development of your knowledge, skills and attitudes.
- Underestimating the importance of personal qualities – 'people buy people first'.
- Becoming too similar to competitors ('me too') instead of creating differences and a competitive edge.
- Losing focus on the real target opportunities for growth of sales and profits – 'fish where the fish are'.

4 Seven inspiring people

- Tom Peters, author of a pioneering series of 'Excellence' books on business. See www.tompeters.com.
- Neil Rackham, author of *Rethinking the Sales Force* (McGraw Hill, 1998). See www.neilrackham.com.
- Theodore Levitt, for his pioneering work in the origins of marketing, including *Marketing Myopia* (Harvard Business Review Classics, 2008).
- James A. Belasco, author of *Teaching the Elephant to Dance* (Century Business, 1990), a leading book on change management in organizations.

- Dr Walter Doyle Staples, author of *Think like a Winner* (Heinemann Asia, 1991), on the value of positive thinking. See www.doctorstaples.com.

- Rosabeth Moss Kantar, author of various books on business entrepreneurship, including *The Change Masters* (Counterpoint, 1983).

- Charles Handy, author of many business books, including *The Empty Raincoat* (Random House Business, 1995) and *The Age of Unreason* (Random House Business, 2002).

5 Seven great quotes

- 'The customer finally decides the fate of an enterprise. This does not mean that other corporate matters are less important, only that they are not more important.' Anonymous

- 'A long journey of 1000 miles begins with a single step.' Chinese philosopher, Laozi (600 BC)

- 'The purpose of a business is to create and keep a customer.' Peter Drucker

- 'The pessimist sees difficulty in every opportunity. The optimist sees opportunity in every difficulty.' Winston Churchill

- 'Ability is what you're capable of doing. Motivation determines what you do. Attitude determines how well you do it.' Lou Holtz, ex-American football coach

- 'Develop the winning edge. Small differences in your performance can lead to large differences in your results.' Brian Tracy, management speaker

- 'The competitor to be feared is the one who goes on making his own business better all the time.'
Henry Ford

6 Seven things to do today

- Ask yourself how you can be a better team member.

- Be honest in asking yourself what value have you added to your specific job today.

- Set an action plan to improve continuously your skills, knowledge and attitude.

- Try to improve your worst characteristic.

- See what you can do to contribute more to the team at meetings.

- Apply the 'so what' test to every decision you take, i.e. ask if you are making a real difference.

- Set yourself a programme to improve your time productivity, i.e. output value relative to work input.

7 Seven trends for tomorrow

- Technology will improve customer and market information, giving more challenges on how to use it.

- Sales forces will decline in number as the marketing and service model is re-engineered in response to market and cost changes.

- The expansion of the Internet channel and social networks will expand electronic commerce.

- Key account management will evolve towards global service/integrated relationships as partnerships become closer between supplier and customers.

- Products and services will be harder to differentiate as globalization produces a trend towards commodities without a competitive edge.

- Profitability will grow in importance over sales in key account management, as companies face increased pressure on margins.

- The need will be for much better qualified key account managers with the trend towards integrated and complex relationships between suppliers and customers.

Answers

Sunday: 1b; 2a,c,d; 3c; 4a,b,c; 5c; 6b,c,d; 7b; 8a,b,c; 9a; 10a,b,d

Monday: 1d; 2c; 3a; 4b;5d; 6b,c; 7a,b,c; 8a,b,c; 9b,c,d; 10a,c,d

Tuesday: 1a,d; 2b; 3b; 4b,c,d; 5b,d; 6c; 7a,c,d; 8a,c; 9a,b; 10a,b

Wednesday: 1a,b,c; 2a,c; 3c; 4b,c,d; 5a,b,c; 6b,c,d; 7a,c; 8b,c; 9b,c,d; 10,b,c,d

Thursday: 1b,c,d; 2a,c; 3b,c; 4b; 5a,d; 6b,c; 7d; 8b,d; 9b,c; 10a,b,c

Friday: 1a,c; 2a,b,d; 3d; 4b,d; 5c,d; 6c; 7c; 8;a,b,c; 9a,c,d; 10a,b,c

Saturday: 1b; 2a,c; 3b; 4a,c; 5b,d; 6a,c,d; 7c; 8a,b,c; 9d; 10a,d

Notes